1985

A HANDBOOK OF
BUSINESS
TERMINOLOGY

A HANDBOOK OF BUSINESS TERMINOLOGY

J. Lyman MacInnis

Chartered Accountant

General Publishing Company
Don Mills, Ontario

First published 1978 by
General Publishing Co. Limited,
30 Lesmill Rd., Don Mills, Ontario

First printing

Canadian Cataloguing in Publication Data

MacInnis, J. Lyman
  Handbook of business terminology

ISBN 0-7736-1042-1

1. Business — Terminology   I. Title

HF1002.M32   650'.03   C78-001318-2

ISBN 0-7736-1042-1
Printed and bound in Canada

Introduction

This is a lexicon of business terminology which defines business terms in layman's language. It is, therefore, a book which *everyone* can use because in the final analysis we are all laymen. The lawyer is a layman when it comes to computer terminology, the computer expert is a layman when confronted by real estate terminology, and the real estate agent is a layman when reading an accounting statement.

In addition to legal, accounting, computer, and real estate terms, this book includes terminology from the fields of economics, taxation, labor, investment, and general commerce as well as commonly used foreign words and phrases.

Students, secretaries, journalists and entrepreneurs will find this book particularly helpful because all the most common terms from the major segments of business are here in one place.

The definitions are expressed in everyday language and not in the stilted jargon of the discipline from which they are drawn. Because of this, some purists might find certain definitions to be imprecise. But remember the purpose of this book — to give the meanings in layman's terms.

Special thanks are due to Darlene Mantini and Margaret Dowling for their assistance in this work.

J. LYMAN MACINNIS C.A.

A HANDBOOK OF
BUSINESS
TERMINOLOGY

a

AFL-CIO: abbreviation for the American Federation of Labor-Congress of Industrial Organizations

AGM: abbreviation for annual general meeting

ALGOL: ALGOrithmic Language, used in computer programming

abandonment: the act of relinguishing ownership of property

abatement: a reduction; often a reduction of taxes provided by statute

ab extra: from outside

ab initio: from the beginning

ab irato: in anger

above par: at a premium

above the line: a phrase indicating a usual revenue or expense item; in contrast to below the line

absenteeism: nonattendance at work for no apparent valid reason

absolute advantage: the ability of a particular country or organization to supply a product or service at a cost lower than that of its competitors

absorption costing: a method of cost accounting in which fixed manufacturing expenses are included in inventory valuation in addition to direct materials, direct labor and variable overhead expenses

abut: to be contiguous to

accelerated depreciation: the allowance of depreciation to be charged against income for tax purposes earlier than would otherwise be the case; normally enacted by governments as an incentive for taxpayers to invest in capital property

acceleration clause: a provision requiring the immediate payment of an unpaid amount upon breach of contract

acceptance paper: promissory notes issued and offered for sale by finance companies

access: the process of obtaining data from or placing data into computer storage

accommodation party: a person who lends his name to help secure credit for another; for example, by signing a note without receiving consideration

account: 1. a statement summarizing transactions over a given period 2. a formal accounting record of a particular (or type of) asset, liability, revenue or expense 3. when plural, the entire set of financial statements of an organization

account executive: an employee, particularly of an advertising agency, who is responsible for all matters relating to a specific client

accounting cycle: the period during which books of account are opened, transactions recorded, financial statements prepared and the books of account closed

accounting period: a period of time for which financial statements are prepared; could be a week, month, quarter or, as is most usual, a year

accounting principle: a rule which has developed and evolved in guiding the measurement, classification and interpretation of activity and information in terms of money. An accounting rule is usually characterized as a principle when no alternative rule is applicable in the circumstances

accounting procedure: the method, chosen by an organization from acceptable alternatives, used in the application of accounting principles

accounting records: books of account, vouchers, and any other documentary evidence used in the accounting function

accounting system: the combination of accounting principles, procedures and records used by a particular organization

accounts payable: amounts due to creditors; usually refers to short-term debts for goods and services rather than long-term liabilities such as bank loans or mortgages

accounts receivable: amounts due from debtors; usually refers to short-term receivables in respect to sales of goods and services rather than long-term debts such as mortgages receivable

accrual accounting: the recording of revenue and expenses as they are earned or incurred rather than when they are received or paid

accrued asset: a receivable which is accumulating with the passage of time or the rendering of services, but which is not yet collectible

accrued expense: an expense which has been incurred in an accounting period but for which no claim for payment can yet be made

accrued interest: interest accumulated since the last interest payment date

accrued liability: a debt which is accumulating with the passage of time or the receipt of services, but which is not yet payable

accrued revenue: revenue which has been earned in an accounting period but for which no claim for payment can yet be made

accumulated depletion: the total to date of periodic depletion charged against income in respect to wasting assets; for example, on a mine, calculated since the particular assets were placed in use

accumulated depreciation: the total to date of periodic depreciation charged against income in respect to depreciable fixed assets calculated since the particular assets were placed in use

acid test: the ratio of total cash, accounts receivable and marketable securities to current liabilities

acquisition: a taking over of one company by another, usually accomplished by purchasing a controlling portion of the other corporation's common stock

across-the-board: applying to everyone or everything

act of God: usually used in connection with damage caused by nature, such as floods, tornados, etc., in contrast to destruction caused by man

actuary: a person who is trained to assess insurance risks in order to advise on the assessing of premiums

added-value tax: synonym for value added tax

ad diem: at the day appointed

ad hoc: for this purpose

ad idem: of the same mind

ad infinitum: indefinitely

adjusting entry: 1. a correcting entry 2. an entry made just before closing the books for an accounting period to apportion items of revenue or expense to accounting periods or various classifications of accounts

administrative expense: an expense of an organization relating to the overall management of its affairs rather than to a particular function

ad rem: to the point

ad valorem: according to value

advance: 1. a payment which is to be accounted for at a later date 2. a loan

advocate: a supporter, in particular a lawyer who pleads on behalf of a client or an accountant who gives testimony on behalf of a client

affidavit: a statement in writing and under oath

affiliated company: a company which is related to another company either through common ownership or as defined by legislation

a fortiori: much more so

after sight: a phrase used in a bill of exchange indicating that the period for which the bill is drawn is to be calculated from the date on which it is first presented to a drawee for acceptance

agenda: a list of items to be discussed at a meeting

agent: a person who acts for a principal in dealings with third parties within terms of reference specified by the principal

aging: the process of analyzing receivables by classification according to the length of time they have been outstanding

algorithm: a series of logically consistent steps that outline a progression of actions which, if followed in order, will lead to the final result

alienation: the transfer from one person to another

alimony: periodic payments, made under a court order for support of a divorced or separated spouse

alio intuito: with a motive other than the admitted one

all fours: an expression indicating that the point at issue is in total agreement with a previous decision

allonge: a paper on which an endorsement is written and attached to and made part of a promissory note

allowance: 1. a reduction or rebate 2. a deduction from the book value of assets to indicate the amount that has been charged to expense 3. an amount paid to an employee or agent to cover expenses, usually a fixed amount which does not have to be accounted for

amalgamation: the combining of two or more corporations by transferring their assets and liabilities to another corporation newly formed for that purpose

amenities: things which increase desirability or enjoyment rather than necessities; for example, in real estate language amenities could include a swimming pool, a panoramic view, etc. In employment terms, amenities could include extra vacation or a luxury office

amicus curiae: literally, a friend of the court; for example, a lawyer who gives information on points of law on which the judge is doubtful

amortization: a gradual and systematic apportioning of an amount over a period of time; for example, the cost of a project might be written off over a period of five years

amortized cost: the original cost of an asset less amounts written off as expenses or losses

analog computer: a computer which performs calculations by the use of electrical or mechanical analogy

analytical auditing: an audit technique based upon an appraisal of an organization's systems of internal control and accounting. The technique relies on a system of flow charting and limited, but in-depth, testing of transactions to determine whether the systems are operating satisfactorily

animus quo: the intention with which

annex: verb: to join a smaller or subordinate thing to a larger or more dominant thing

annexation: permanently affixing, such as a city increasing its size by adding additional land in its jurisdiction

annual report: the information, usually consisting of financial statements and reports of the organization's directors and/or officers, presented annually by the directors and/or management to shareholders and other interested parties

annuity certain: an annuity payable for a fixed number of years whether or not the beneficiary lives that long

annul: to make void

ante: before

antedate: to put a date on a document earlier than that on which it was issued

antedated: a document or check that is dated sometime in the past

a posteriori: from the effect to the cause

appellant: the party filing an appeal

applied overhead: overhead costs which have been allocated to a particular product or activity

appraisal: a valuation made by qualified experts

appreciation: increase in value

apprentice: a person who has contracted to work for an employer for a fixed period of time in order to learn a skill and gain practical experience

appropriation: 1. in government accounting, an approval estimate representing the maximum of funds authorized for a purpose but which does not of itself represent approval for actual expenditures 2. an authorization with specific time and amount limitations 3. a transfer of retained earnings or net income to a reserve in order to limit distribution

appurtenance: in real estate language, something belonging to something else, such as a garage to a house

a priori: from the cause to the effect

a quo: from which

arbitrage: a simultaneous purchase and sale of identical commodities, foreign currencies, or securities in different markets in order to profit from price differences

arbitration: a method of settling disputes out of court through the intervention of a third party (or parties) whose decision is final and binding

arbitrator: a person selected to settle a disagreement out of court

architect's certificate: formal documentation by an architect that a contractor has performed as required under a contract and is entitled to be paid

arm's length: a situation in which the parties to a transaction are not related or closely connected with each other

arrears: interest or dividends which were not paid when due

as is: a condition of sale under which the buyer accepts the property in the exact condition existing at the time of the sale

ask: the price a potential seller asks for a stock, bond or other asset

assay: a test conducted to determine the proportion of precious metal in an ore

assessment roll: the list of taxable persons and property in a particular jurisdiction as compiled by the official assessors

assessor: one who estimates values for tax purposes

asset: something of value

asset-poor: the condition of being short of money because of owning an excess of properties which don't produce income

assignment: a transfer of property, or a right or interest therein, by one person to another to be used by the latter for his own benefit, for the benefit of creditors, or to be held in trust

associated company or corporation: 1. an entity operating in cooperation with another by reason of common ownership or by agreement 2. an entity associated with another as defined by legislation

assumption of mortgage: in taking title to a property, the assumption of personal liability for an existing mortgage

assurance: a synonym for insurance

attorney-in-fact: a person holding a power of attorney as an agent for another person

attrition: reduction through natural causes

audi alteram partem: hear the other side; which is to say, no one should be condemned unheard

audit: 1. an examination of the accounting records and other supporting evidence of an organization for the purpose of expressing an opinion as to whether the organization's financial statements present fairly both its financial position as at a particular date and the results of its operations for the period ending on that date in accordance with generally accepted accounting principles 2. an examination of evidence to determine reliability

audit committee: a committee, selected from among the directors of an organization, whose specific functions are to review the annual financial statements before they are presented to the full board of directors and to act as a liaison between the board and the organization's auditors

auditing procedures: the steps carried out by an auditor in applying auditing techniques to particular circumstances

auditing standards: standards which have evolved against which the appropriateness of auditing procedures are measured in relation to the desired objectives of the audit

auditing techniques: the methods of obtaining audit evidence

auditor: one who performs an audit

auditor's certificate: synonym for auditor's report

auditor's report: any report by an auditor in accordance with the terms of his engagement, but usually refers to the formal expression of the auditor's opinion as to whether the financial statements of an organization present fairly both its financial position as at a particular date and the results of its operations for the period ending on that date in accordance with generally accepted accounting principles

audit trail: the means by which the processing of data can be traced through the processing cycle

authorized capital: the number and par value, if any, of shares of each class of the capital stock that a corporation can issue in accordance with its documents of incorporation

autocracy: an organizational structure in which one person has power over all others in the organization

autocrat: a person who exercises power over all others in an organization

automation: technical developments which allow the replacement of human operations with machines

autonomy: the condition which exists when one has the right to organize one's affairs without external interference

average cost: the determination of the cost of an item by dividing the total cost of such items by the number of units at a point in time or over a period of time

backlog: unfilled orders

back order: the unfilled portion of an original order for goods or services

back pay: wages due for past services

bad debt: an account or loan receivable that is considered to be uncollectible

bad debts recovered: amounts collected which had previously been written off as bad debts

balance of payments: the net result of a nation's transactions with the outside world over a particular period of time

balance of trade: the difference between the value of exports and imports over a given period of time

balance sheet: a statement showing the assets, liabilities and owner's equity of a person, partnership, corporation or other entity at a particular point in time

balloon: the last payment on a balloon note

balloon note: a note calling for periodic payments which are not large enough to pay off the face amount of the note prior to maturity so that a large final payment known as the balloon is due when the note matures

bank confirmation: a statement which an auditor obtains from a client's bank detailing the position of the client's balances, loans and other matters as at a particular date

bank reconciliation: a statement accounting for the difference between a bank balance per the bank statement and the balance for the same account as reflected in the books of account of the bank's customer for the same date

bankrupt: the legal status of a person who has made an assignment in bankruptcy. In general terms it means being in a state of financial ruin

bankruptcy: the state of being bankrupt

bargaining agent: a union designated by legislation as the exclusive representative of all employees in a particular bargaining unit for the purpose of collective bargaining

bargaining unit: a group of workers in a particular industry, department, plant, craft or occupation who have been determined under legislation as appropriate for purposes of collective bargaining

barratry: the misdemeanor of habitually starting quarrels or nuisance litigation

barter: an exchange of goods or services for other goods or services rather than for cash

batch: a number of records or documents considered as a single unit for the purpose of data processing

bear: one who believes that prices will fall and sells in anticipation of that event

bearer security: a security not registered in the name of a particular owner or on which the last endorsement is blank so that physical possession of the security may establish ownership

bearish: a market in which the prevailing trend of prices is downward; an attitude that prices are about to fall

beggar-my-neighbor: a method of increasing the exports of one country at the expense of those of other countries

below the line: an item of revenue or expense of an unusual character; usually used only in connection with large amounts

benchmark: a measurement by which others are compared

beneficial owner: the real owner of something

benefit-based pension plan: a plan under which the pension benefits are determined in accordance with years of service and amounts earned by the employee

bid: the price a prospective buyer offers for a stock, bond or other asset

big board: a nickname for the New York Stock Exchange

big business: any business enterprise which is large in relation to the market in which it operates

bill of exchange: an unconditional order in writing, addressed by one person to another, signed by the person giving it, requiring the person to whom it is addressed to pay, at a fixed or determinable future time or on demand, a certain sum of money to, or to the order of, the bearer or any other specified person

bill of lading: a document executed by common carriers acknowledging the receipt of goods and which serves as a document of title to the goods consigned

bill of materials: specifications of the quantity and type of materials entering into a particular product or structure

binary: a type of mathematics where the numerical form uses the base two rather than the base ten

bin card: an inventory card showing the actual quantity of goods in a bin or other receptacle or on a shelf. The card is corrected each time material is added or removed

black market: the illegal purchase and sale of scarce commodities, usually at prices well above fair market value

blank check: a check that is signed by the maker but which does not have an amount filled in

blanket policy: an insurance policy that covers all the property insured against loss under one sum without the itemizing of separate values for each individual item

blocked currency: currency which by force of law cannot be expatriated or exchanged for the currency of another country

block trade: a transaction involving an unusually large number of shares

blue chip stocks: shares in well-established companies, normally with a long and satisfactory dividend record and all the attributes of a perfectly safe investment

blue-collar workers: a term applied to production and maintenance workers in contrast to office and professional personnel

blue-sky law: a term for a law regulating the issue of securities

board lots: the number of shares in a corporation which represents a regular trading unit as decided upon by a stock exchange

board of directors: a committee of persons elected by the eligible members of an organization to be responsible for managing its affairs; for example, the body elected by the shareholders of a corporation

board of trade: a synonym for chamber of commerce

boiler room: the peddling of stocks, usually of doubtful value, over the telephone

bona fide: in good faith; genuine

bona vacantia: goods without an apparent owner

bond: 1. a certificate of indebtedness, usually implying that assets have been pledged as security 2. an indemnity against loss caused by a third party

bond discount: the amount by which the selling price of a bond is less than its face value

bond premium: the amount by which the selling price of a bond exceeds its face value

bonded goods: goods on which excise or customs duties must be paid

bonded warehouse: a warehouse in which goods are stored without excise or customs duties being paid until they are removed from the warehouse

book debt: a synonym for an account payable or receivable, as the case might be

book of original entry: a book of account in which transactions are recorded for the first time; for example, a journal which will be summarized and posted to other accounting ledgers

bookkeeping: the classification and recording of business transactions in terms of money

book profit: unrealized profit

book value: the amount at which an item appears in the accounting records or on financial statements. Without knowing the exact basis on which it is determined, it is a meaningless figure

boom: a time during which the economy is working at or close to full capacity with resources being fully utilized and prices rising rapidly

boot: something given in addition

borough: a political subdivision of a city, having authority over certain local matters

the bottom line: a phrase indicating the final result, such as the net profit after taxes

bourgeoisie: the middle-class group in society

boycott: a campaign designed to urge people not to purchase goods or services produced by a particular company, industry or country

brainstorming: a creative technique under which a problem is presented to a group of people who then state their ideas immediately and as often as they come to mind with the view that the many answers provided will include an appropriate one

brand name: any combination of letters or words used by one manufacturer or supplier to distinguish his goods and services from those of other companies

break-even point: point where revenue equals expenses

break-up value: the net amount which would be realized upon the winding up of a business

bridge financing: an interim loan made for a short period during which the borrower is arranging long-term financing

broker: generally an agent who acts for both parties to a transaction

brokerage fees: the fees, usually a commission, charged by a broker

broom clean: in real estate language, used to describe the condition of a building turned over to a buyer or tenant with the floors swept and completely free of debris

bucket shop: an operation by a broker in which customers' orders are not immediately processed but are held with the possibility that a price change will afford the broker a personal gain

budget: an estimate of future transactions

budget deficit: an excess of expenses over revenues

budget surplus: an excess of revenues over expenses

building permit: a permit granted by a local government enabling the holder to construct or renovate a building

bull: one who believes that prices will go up and who invests his money in securities or other property and advises others to do so

bullion: precious metal in the form of bars. Sometimes also refers to large quantities of coins

bullish: a market in which the prevailing trend of prices is upward; an attitude that prices are about to rise

bumping: in labor language, the practice under which one worker is allowed to replace another worker in a job because the former has greater seniority

burst: the separation of individual sheets from a continuous form

business barometer: a weighted average of a variety of economic indicators

business days: all days other than Saturday, Sunday and legal holidays

business interruption insurance: insurance against continuing expenses or loss of earnings resulting from interruption of business caused by an insured risk, such as fire

bust: a drop in business activity to an exceptionally low level

buyers' market: when supply exceeds demand

by-laws: the rules and regulations adopted by an organization to regulate its internal operations

by-product: a marketable product of lesser importance produced incidentally with a major product

C

C.A.: abbreviation for Chartered Accountant

C.G.A.: abbreviation for Certified General Accountant

c.i.f.: abbreviation for cost, insurance, freight. A condition of sale under which the price includes the cost of handling, insurance, and freight, delivered to a particular location

CLC: abbreviation for the Canadian Labour Congress, Canada's national labor body which represents almost three-quarters of organized labor in Canada

CLU: abbreviation for Canada Life Underwriter

COBOL: COmmon Business Oriented Language, used in computer programming

c.o.d.: cash on delivery

C.P.A.: abbreviation for Certified Public Accountant

call: a transferable option to buy a specific number of shares of a particular stock at a stated price at any time during the stated period

canceled check: a check that has been honored by the bank on which it was drawn and on which evidence of payment is stamped or otherwise indicated

capital: 1. in a corporation, that portion of the equity which is contributed by the shareholders 2. the interest of the owners of a business; that is, the excess of assets over liabilities 3. owners' equity 4. the total funds provided by lenders and owners for use by a business

capital asset: an asset intended for long-term use

capital cost allowance: the income tax term for depreciation

capital expenditure: the cost of acquiring a capital asset

capital flight: a massive transfer of currency out of a country because of adverse economic, political, or military policies

capital gain: in general terms, the profit made on the sale of a capital asset. However, under income tax law the term has a special meaning

capital-intensive industry: an industry that utilizes extraordinarily large amounts of assets in relation to its labor force

capitalism: an economic system which encourages privately owned and directed production, distribution, and marketing

capitalize: to treat an expenditure as a capital asset rather than an expense. Capitalized costs might or might not be written off over a period of time

capital loss: the opposite of capital gain

capital stock: the ownership interest in a corporation as authorized by the terms of its incorporation

carrying charges: usually refers to interest

carte blanche: without restriction

cartel: a group of separate business organizations that has banded together and agreed to institute measures which will effectively control competition

case study: an account of events and factors relating to a particular business problem

cash basis accounting: the recording of revenue and expenses as they are received or paid rather than when earned or incurred. The opposite of accrual accounting

cash book: a book of original entry used for recording cash received and cash paid out

cash discount: a reduction of a debt granted by a creditor in consideration of payment within a particular time period

cash flow: the cash position of an enterprise determined under cash basis accounting

cashier's check: a check drawn by a bank against itself rather than against the customer's account. They are usually sold to customers for remittance purposes. Normally a cashier's check does not show the name of the person who purchased it

cash surrender value: the amount which would be received upon cancellation of an insurance policy

casting vote: an additional vote granted to the chairman of a meeting to be used if the votes cast for and against a particular resolution (including the chairman's ordinary vote) are tied. A casting vote is not an automatic right, it must be given to the chairman by the constitution of the organization

casus omissus: a point not provided for

cats and dogs: highly speculative, low-priced issues of shares

causa causans: the immediate cause

central bank: a bank set up by a government to transact government business and to recommend and implement the government's monetary policy

certificate of deposit: a fixed-income debt security issued by chartered banks. Their terms are normally one to six years

certified check: a check bearing evidence on its face that payment of it is guaranteed by the bank on which it is drawn

certiorari: writ from a higher court for records of a case tried in lower court

cestui que trust: a beneficiary

chain store: a unit in a group of retail stores of the same general type, commonly owned and with a degree of centralized control over operations

chamber of commerce: an organization of businessmen in a particular area formed to promote commerce and industry in that area

charter: the instrument of incorporation

charter party: a contract under which a ship is leased

chattel mortgage: a mortgage secured by a chattel or chattels

chattels: tangible, personal property other than real property

check: a bill of exchange drawn on a bank, payable on demand

checklist: a series of questions or instructions to be followed in particular circumstances

check-off system: the system under which union dues are collected from employees by having the employer make deductions directly from wages and remit the amounts to the union

check register: a book of original entry in which the details of checks issued are recorded

chose in action: the right to possession rather than possession itself

circulating capital: a synonym for working capital

civil action: a legal action which is not a criminal action

class action suit: a lawsuit in which the plaintiff is a group of all persons who share some identifying and common characteristic, such as all owners of a particular make of automobile

clearing account: an account in which amounts are entered until such time as they are more accurately classified and transferred to other accounts

clearing house: an organization acting as a medium for the daily settlement of transactions between its members

closed-end: a capital structure of an organization under which shares are transferable but cannot be canceled or redeemed except by resolution of the shareholders or under legislation

closed-end fund: an investment company with fixed capital and no provision for redemption of shares at the option of the shareholders

closed shop: where a worker must be a member of a union in order to be employed and all employees must be hired through the union

closely-held corporation: a corporation in which the shares are held by a small number of shareholders

closing: the final procedure in which documents are executed and recorded

closing costs: expenses incidental to the sale of real estate

closing entry: an entry made at the end of an accounting period for the purpose of transferring the balances in the revenue and expense accounts to retained earnings or similar accounts

closing statement: the statement which lists the financial settlement between a buyer and a seller outlining the amounts each must pay

cloud on title: an encumbrance, usually invalid, on real property

codicil: a document, executed in the same manner as the will itself, which alters a will

co-insurance: a stipulation in an insurance contract under which the insured must maintain his insurance at an agreed percentage of the value of the thing insured or, alternatively, to contribute proportionately to his own loss

cola: an abbreviation for cost of living allowance

collate: to sort into a meaningful order

collateral: security

collective agreement: a contract between one or more unions and one or more employers

collective bargaining: a method of determining conditions of employment through direct negotiations between the union and the employer

comfort letter: a letter by which the writer conveys assurance that something is or is not so to the best of the writer's knowledge

commercial paper: although sometimes restricted to short-term promissory notes issued by corporations, the term also applies to checks, drafts, and other negotiable instruments

common area: the area owned in common, such as walkways, hallways, etc., by the owners of condominiums

common carrier: a person or company in the business of transporting goods and passengers for anyone who wishes to use the services, in contrast to being under an exclusive contract

common share: a synonym for common stock

common stock: capital stock other than preferred stock. It is the common stockholders who normally control a corporation's operation and are entitled to ultimate ownership of its retained earnings

communism: a political and economic system under which all of a country's means of production and distribution are owned and controlled by the state

community property: in jurisdictions having community property laws, such as Quebec and California, property owned in common by a husband and wife, which property was not acquired as separate property

company law: law which applies to corporations

company seal: the official seal of a corporation which must be affixed to or imprinted on certain documents

comparative statement: a form of financial statement presentation in which current period results and positions are presented with corresponding figures for previous periods

compensating balance: money deposited in a bank or other lending institution to induce the institution to make a specific loan or establish a particular line of credit. Sometimes such deposits are made by third parties rather than the party applying for the loan

compensating errors: errors which happen to cancel each other out

competent: having the necessary age, ability, and authority to contract

completed contract method: a method of accounting which recognizes income only when the goods to be provided or the services to be rendered have been provided or rendered as the case might be

compound interest: interest calculated on interest accumulated as well as on the principal amount of a loan

comptroller: a synonym for controller

compulsory arbitration: arbitration imposed by law on parties to a dispute

computer: an electronic device which is capable of accepting information, applying prescribed processes to such information and supplying the results of these processes

computer program: a set of instructions which tells the computer what to do

computer run: the processing of a batch of transactions. Sometimes restricted to the performance of one routine or several interconnected routines

computer software: the computer programs used to activate and instruct the computer system in contrast to the actual processing equipment

computer terminal: a point at which data can be put into or extracted from a computer system

concession: the granting of a right

conciliation: in labor language, a process which attempts to resolve labor disputes by compromise or voluntary agreement in contrast to arbitration

conditional discharge: the release of a bankrupt from his liabilities subject to the fulfillment of specified conditions

conditional sales agreement: a contract of sale under which the transfer of title does not take place until specified payments have been made

condition precedent: a condition which must be met before a contract becomes binding

condominium: the term describing individual ownership in real property of a specific unit of a multi-unit structure

conference board: an independent, nonprofit organization found in several countries which studies the social, economic and business problems of the country and disseminates facts and conclusions based on its investigation

configuration: a group of interconnected machines which are programmed to operate as one system

con man: a person who creates unreasonable confidence in his honesty and integrity

consensus: general agreement by a number of people

consent judgment: an agreement between a plaintiff and a defendant to have a particular judgment entered and recorded

consideration: something of value given. *See also* **valuable consideration**

consignment: a shipment of goods under an agreement whereby the receiving party undertakes to sell them as an agent for the shipper. The shipper retains title to the goods until they are sold

console: the control keys and special devices unit of a computer

consolidated financial statements: the combined financial statements of a parent company and its subsidiaries

consortium: an association of independent organizations usually formed to undertake a specific project that requires skill and resources which are not possessed by any of the participants individually

constant dollars: dollars of a given base year into which dollars of the year under review are restated for the purpose of eliminating the change in purchasing power

consumer credit: credit extended to individuals to enable them to obtain goods and services for their own personal use

consumer price index: a monthly measure compiled by the government of changes in the prices of selected goods and services consumed by individuals

consumption: the expenditure of a nation or its individuals on consumer goods and services. Expenditures on capital goods are not considered in determining consumption

contingency fund: amounts set aside for unforeseen expenditures

contingent asset: something of potential value depending on the occurrence or nonoccurrence of a specific future event

contingent liability: a legal obligation which may arise in the future out of past or present circumstances provided certain developments take place

contra account: an account that offsets in whole or in part another account

contract: an agreement between persons having the legal capacity to bind themselves to do a lawful thing for valuable consideration

contributed capital: paid-up capital plus contributed surplus

contributed surplus: 1. the amount received on the issue of par value shares in excess of the par value; the portion of proceeds received for no par value shares that has been allocated to surplus; the proceeds of sale of donated shares, the profit on forfeited shares, amounts contributed by shareholders, or any other contributions made by shareholders in excess of the stated value of shares 2. capital donations from sources other than shareholders

contributory pension plan: a pension plan under which the costs are shared between the employer and the employee

control account: a general ledger account representing the total of the balances of the accounts in a subsidiary ledger

controlled company: a corporation which is under the control of another corporation or person

controller: an officer of an organization with the technical skills of an accountant who is charged with the responsibility for administration of financial matters

controlling account: a synonym for control account

controlling interest: the shares held by a controlling shareholder or shareholders

controlling shareholder(s): a shareholder or group of shareholders owning sufficient shares to elect a majority of the board of directors of a corporation

conveyance: the transfer of title to land from one person to another

conventional mortgage: a mortgage not obtained under a government insured program

conversion: the unlawful taking of or possession of goods of another

conversion cost: usually refers to the cost of transforming raw materials into finished products but could be used to refer to the cost of changing any existing resource from one form or function to another

convertible: 1. in relation to currency, capable of being exchanged for the currency of another country 2. in relation to securities, capable of being exchanged for securities of another class

cooling-off period: in labor language, a period during which employees cannot strike and employers cannot engage in a lockout. During this time it is hoped the dispute may be settled

cooperative: an organization formed for the benefit of its owners who are usually either producers or consumers; the concept being that by cooperating they acquire profits which would otherwise go to middlemen

copyright: the exclusive right to produce or reproduce an original literary, dramatic, musical or artistic work. Usually the term of copyright protection is for the life of the author and fifty years after his death. These rights are confirmed by the Copyright Act

coram: in the presence of

corner: the buying of a stock or commodity on a scale sufficiently large to give the buyers control over the price of the particular stock or commodity

corporate image: the opinion that the public holds of a particular corporation

corporation: a legal entity, with or without share capital, separate and distinct from its owners, which has all the rights and responsibilities of a natural person (except those rights which only a natural person can exercise) whose owners are liable for corporate debts only up to the amount of their investment

corporeal: tangible

cost accounting: the branch of accounting which concerns itself with the classification, recording, analysis, reporting and interpretation of expenditures in connection with the production and distribution of goods and services

cost-based pension plan: a synonym for a money-purchase pension plan

cost-benefit study or analysis: evaluating the benefits to be expected from a project, determining the cost of the project, then making a decision whether to proceed based on the comparison of the two

cost center: a unit within an organization with which costs are identified for purposes of management control

cost method: a means of accounting for investments in other corporations under which the investment is recorded at cost, and post-acquisition earnings of the investee are recorded only to the extent that they are received as dividends

cost of capital: the cost of investment funds whether obtained through borrowing, equity investment or retained earnings; usually expressed in terms of yield

cost of goods sold: the total cost of goods sold during an accounting period

cost-of-living allowance: an automatic periodic pay increase based on changes in the consumer price index

cost-plus contract: a contract under which the contractor recovers costs incurred in performance plus an agreed fee

cost-push inflation: the theory that inflation is caused by workers demanding higher wages without increase in productivity followed by employers raising prices without an increase in demand

countersign: to sign one's signature to a document that has already been signed by someone else, often as a guarantee of authenticity

coupon bond: a bond having detachable coupons which are presented to the issuer for payment of interest on specified due dates

covenant: an agreement or promise contained in a legal document that something is or shall be or as to the truth of a particular fact or facts

credit bureau: an organization that compiles and supplies information about the reliability of individuals or companies in the payment of their debts

credit line: an arrangement with a bank under which the bank agrees, usually informally, to make a loan not to exceed a particular amount when needed by the customer

credit note: a document prepared by a seller of goods or services notifying a purchaser that the latter's account is being reduced because of an allowance, return, cancellation or similar event

creditor: one to whom something is owed

credit report: a report issued by a credit bureau or other investigating agency giving information about an individual or corporation which is intended to influence a decision whether to grant credit

credit squeeze: a restriction by a government on the provision of credit to consumers

credit union: a savings and loan institution organized on a cooperative basis to provide savings and loan services to and for the benefit of its member owners

crown corporation: a corporation which is accountable for the conduct of its affairs to the federal or a provincial government

cul de sac: a dead end street

cum div: a quoted price which includes a declared but unpaid dividend

cumulative dividends: dividends at a fixed annual rate on preferred stock which, if not paid in a particular year, are carried forward and added to the dividends which the preferred shareholders are entitled to in the future

cumulative stock: a class of preferred stock on which unpaid dividends continue to accumulate

curia: a court of justice

current account: a running account; usually refers to an account in which a significant number of entries are made and in which the balance fluctuates

current assets: cash or other assets that in the normal course of operations would be expected to be converted into cash or consumed in the production of income within one year, or within the normal operating cycle of the business if that is longer than a year

current liability: a liability which it is expected will be paid within one year or within an organization's normal operating cycle where that is longer than a year

current ratio: the ratio of current assets to current liabilities

current service pension cost: the pension cost which relates to an employee's employment after a pension plan is put into effect in contrast to costs relating to his service in prior years

current value accounting: a general term used to describe methods of accounting based on current values rather than historical cost

curriculum vitae: a resumé of one's qualifications and career

d

damages: indemnification for loss

data bank: an organized file of information

data center: a data processing installation serving several users or customers; usually restricted to computerized operations

data processing: the assembly, classification, recording, analysis and reporting of information by manual, mechanical or electronic means

days of grace: additional days, usually three, allowed beyond the due date of a payment during which payment can still be made

debasement: the act of reducing the metallic content of a coin below its face value

debenture: a certificate of indebtedness, usually implying an unsecured obligation

debit: an entry recording the creation of, or addition to, an asset or an expense, or the reduction of a liability, revenue, or owners' equity

debit memorandum: a synonym for debit note

debit note: a document prepared by a purchaser notifying a seller that the latter's account has been reduced because of an allowance, return or cancellation

debt: a sum of money owing

decision tree: a diagram of a sequence of decisions each of which involves choosing between alternatives depending on the results of previous decisions

declaration: 1. any formal document attesting a fact 2. in relation to a dividend, the formal act of a corporation creating a liability to pay a dividend

decreasing term insurance: a form of term insurance under which the face amount of insurance decreases each year

decree: an order of a court

decree absolute: the final decree of a court

decree nisi: a decree which is not made absolute until after a specified period

deed: a written instrument executed and delivered under which title or interest in real property is conveyed from one person to another

deem: consider to be

de facto: in fact

defalcation: a form of embezzlement, usually restricted to absconding with cash

default: to omit to do that which by law a person is required to do

deferred annuity: an annuity under which payments are not due to begin until some years in the future even though the premium is payable now

deferred income: an amount of income received or receivable but not yet earned

deficit: the opposite of a surplus

de jure: by right

delist: to remove a security from the list of those traded on a major stock exchange

delisted stock: a security which has been removed from the list of those traded on a major stock exchange

demand loan: a loan which must be repaid whenever the lender requests repayment rather than at a stated time

demand-pull inflation: a theory holding that inflation is caused by an excess of demand for goods over the economy's ability to supply them. Prices go up, the level of wages follows causing an increase in demand for goods, and the cycle continues

demurrage: a charge by a common carrier for loading, unloading, or storage time in excess of agreed limits

de novo: new

depletion: a charge in an accounting period to reflect the estimated cost of the portion of wasting assets, such as timber or the output of a mine, consumed or removed during that period

deponent: a person who gives evidence

depose: to make a statement on oath

deposit: 1. a lodgment of cash, securities, etc., with another party, such as depositing money in a bank 2. a synonym for down payment

deposit certificate: a document certifying that a deposit of a specific amount has been made with a financial institution for a specified period of time and at a specified rate of interest

deposit insurance: insurance on deposits made to a financial institution, protecting the depositor from loss up to a stated amount should the financial institution fail

depreciated cost: original cost less accumulated depreciation

depreciation: decrease in value; usually refers to the charge in an accounting period to reflect the estimated loss of value of fixed assets through use and obsolescence

devaluation: the lowering of the value of a nation's currency in relation to the currency of other countries

developing nation: a nation whose people are beginning to utilize their resources in order to bring about an increase in production of goods and services

dictum: an opinion of a judge

die without issue: having no children at the date of death

digital computer: a computer which handles data in the form of discrete digits

diminishing balance method: a method of calculating depreciation in which the periodic charge is computed as a constant percentage of the depreciated cost; for example, applying a percentage of ten percent each year to the depreciated cost so that the depreciation charged reduces each year

direct cost: an item of cost that can reasonably be identified with a specific operation or other cost center

direct costing: a method of cost accounting in which only direct materials, direct labor, and variable overhead expenses are charged to inventory. Under this method fixed manufacturing expenses are considered to be period costs and are not included in inventory valuation

direct labor: the cost of labor applied to the materials that will form an integral part of a final product in a manufacturing process

direct material: the cost of material forming an integral part of a final product in a manufacturing process

direct offering: the public offering of a security issued through the issuer's own facilities rather than through investment dealers

direct overhead: overhead costs traceable to a specific part of an operation

disbursement: an outlay of cash

discharge: to relieve of an obligation or responsibility

disclaimer: a denial

discount: 1. a reduction from a list price 2. the amount by which the selling price of a security is less than its par value 3. an amount deducted as interest in advance from the face value of a note when it is sold for its present worth 4. any difference between present value and value at maturity of a security 5. as a verb, to sell a security for its present value 6. as a verb, to compute the present value of a future sum

discounted cash flow: a method of calculating return on an investment which takes into consideration the changing value of money over time

discounted value: the value at a given date of a future amount determined by applying compound interest at a given rate to the payment of the future amount

discretionary account: in stock market language, an account established by a customer with a broker for the purchase and sale of securities under which the broker is authorized to exercise his own discretion with respect to the securities purchased or sold as well as the time and price of the transactions

discretionary order: an order given to a broker specifying the stock or commodity and the quantity to be bought or sold, but leaving to the judgment of the broker the time and the price of the transaction

display console: a visual display unit of a computer, similar to a television screen

disposable income: an individual's income after taxes

distribution costs: a synonym for selling costs, such as advertising, storage, delivery, etc.

diversified company: a corporation engaged in several different lines of business either directly or through subsidiary companies

dividend: 1. profits distributed to shareholders of a corporation 2. an amount distributed to shareholders of a corporation upon liquidation 3. a patronage return to the members of a cooperative or credit union 4. a rebate of life insurance premiums 5. an amount distributed to the creditors on a pro rata basis out of the net amount realized in a bankruptcy

donatio mortis causa: a gift in contemplation of death

donee: a person who receives a gift

donor: a person who makes a gift

dormant company: an inactive company which continues to comply with legal requirements to continue its existence

doubtful debt: an amount receivable which may not be collectible

dower: a wife's right to a portion of the real property held by her husband during their marriage

Dow Jones averages: stock price averages computed by Dow Jones & Company, publishers of the *Wall Street Journal*, giving the average stock prices by class based on the highest, lowest, opening, and closing stock price averages for representative issues. The most commonly used average is the average of thirty industrial stocks, all of which are listed on the New York Stock Exchange

draft: a bill of exchange

drawings: withdrawals of cash or merchandise from a business by a sole proprietor or partner

dumping: the practice of selling goods below generally recognized market prices while maintaining higher prices in other areas where government protection or other preferred treatment is available

duopoly: a market structure in which there are only two sellers of a commodity or service

durable goods: goods with a normal life expectancy of three years or more, such as automobiles or furniture

dura lex sed lex: severe law, but law

Dutch auction: a form of auction where the auctioneer begins the bidding at a very high price and reduces it until he gets a bid

e

EDP: abbreviation for electronic data processing

e. & o.e.: errors and omissions excepted

earnest money: a deposit made with a view to creating a binding agreement

earnings per share: a corporation's income for a period divided by the number of shares outstanding at the end of the period which are entitled to full participation in the earnings

easement: the right enjoyed by one owner of real property over the real property of another person; for example, a right-of-way

easy money: money that can be borrowed at very low interest rates

Economic Council of Canada: an organization, independent from government, the aim of which is to plot the potential growth and prospective problems in the Canadian economy in order to assist forward planning

economy of scale: the condition that exists when the average cost of production declines as output increases

effective tax rate: the average rate of taxation; total tax payable divided by the income on which the tax was calculated

ejusdem generis: of the same kind

eliminating entries: adjustments in the preparation of consolidated financial statements made to prevent duplication due to intercompany transactions

embargo: a government order stopping the import or export of a particular commodity or commodities

embezzlement: misappropriation of assets in one's custody and control

emblements: growing crops

emoluments: total payment for work done or services provided

empirical: based on experience

en bloc: as a unit

encroachment: in real estate language, the construction onto the property of another

encumbrance: a lien against real or personal property

endowment fund: property, usually cash or securities donated or bequeathed to a charitable, religious, educational, or other non-profit institution, the income from which is used by the institution according to the conditions attached to the gifts. The principal must be maintained intact or applied only as set out in the conditions attached to the gift

endowment insurance: a type of life insurance under which payment of the amount of the insurance is made upon the death of the insured or upon the end of a specified period of time, whichever occurs first

engagement letter: a letter from a public accountant to a client outlining the scope of the accountant's responsibilities and the arrangements agreed upon with respect to a particular engagement

entrepreneur: a person who, on his own initiative, establishes and operates a business enterprise

eo instanti: at that instant

equal pay: pay that is the same for all people performing the same work

equitable title: ownership by a person who does not have legal title

equity: the residual interest of an owner after all relevant debts have been paid

equity method: a basis of accounting for investments in other corporations under which the investment is initially recorded at cost and the carrying value is adjusted thereafter to show the investor's pro rata share of the post-acquisition earnings of the investee

escalation clause: a clause in a contract which permits upward adjustments of price under specified conditions

escape clause: a provision allowing one or more parties to a contract to withdraw therefrom or to modify their performance provided stipulated conditions exist

escheat: the reversion of property to the state by failure of persons legally entitled to hold the property to lay claim to it

escrow: the state of something being held in trust by a person who is not a party to the matter until such time as certain conditions are met

escrowed shares: shares of a corporation which, while still entitled to vote and receive dividends, cannot be bought or sold without special approval being obtained from the party whose interest the escrow is designed to protect

estate planning: the arrangement of a person's affairs to facilitate the passage of his assets to his beneficiaries and to minimize taxes upon death

estimated cost system: a method of cost accounting in which the costs of production are initially based on estimated costs with adjustments later for differences between estimated and actual costs

et al: and others

et seq: and following

Eurodollar: a U.S. dollar held outside the United States, particularly in Europe

European Common Market: an economic union for trade purposes consisting of: Italy, the Federal Republic of Germany, Belgium, Luxembourg, France, the Netherlands, Great Britain and Greece

examination for discovery: the pre-trial examination and cross-examination under oath of the parties to an action enabling both the plaintiff and defendant to assess each other's case

ex cathedra: with high authority

excise tax: a tax charged on goods produced or manufactured

exclusive listing: in real estate language, an agreement between a property owner and a real estate agent under which the owner must pay a commission to the agent if the property in question is sold during the listing period regardless of whether the agent is the cause of the sale

ex contractu: arising from a contract

ex delicto: arising out of wrongs

ex div: a quoted price which does not include a declared but unpaid dividend

execution: the signing of written documents making them legally valid

executor: a person appointed under a will to administer the affairs of the deceased

exemplary damages: damages awarded by a court in excess of the amount needed to compensate the plaintiff in order to punish the wrongdoer

ex gratia: voluntary

ex mero motu: of one's own free will

ex officio: officially; by virtue of an office

ex parte: on behalf of

expert testimony: testimony given by one acknowledged to have special training and knowledge of a particular subject

expert witness: one who is acknowledged to have special training and knowledge of a particular subject

ex post facto: by a subsequent act

expropriation: the right of the state to take private real property for public use with compensation being given to the owner

ex rel: on the information of

extended coverage: in insurance language, coverage beyond the normal, standard policy

effective rate: the actual rate of return on an investment in contrast to the stated rate; for example a $100 bond with an interest rate of ten percent would yield an effective rate of 11.1 percent if the bond was purchased for $90

f.a.s.: abbreviation for free along side, a condition of sale under which the price of goods includes all costs until the goods are placed along side the vehicle in which they are to be shipped

F.C.A.: abbreviation for Fellow of the Institute of Chartered Accountants

F.C.I.S.: abbreviation for Fellow of the Institute of Chartered Secretaries and Administrators

FIFO: first in first out

f.o.b.: an abbreviation for free on board, a condition of sale under which the price of goods includes all charges until the goods are placed on the vehicle on which they are to be shipped and the vehicle is at or reaches a specified place

FORTRAN: FORmula TRANslating system; a computer language

face value: the value of a bond or other security that appears on its face; usually the amount which the issuer promises to pay at maturity

facsimile signatures: signatures on checks, stock certificates, bonds or other documents which are mechanically imprinted

factor: a person who buys receivables at a discount from another to provide the other person with cash or to relieve the other person of the risk of collecting the receivables

fair market value: the amount which a willing buyer would pay and a willing seller would accept in an open and unrestricted market assuming that both parties are knowledgeable, deal at arm's length, and neither is under any compulsion to act

fait accompli: something that is done; an accomplished fact

feasibility study: an investigation before the commencement of a project to determine the probable success thereof

featherbedding: the provision under union pressure of employment for more workers than are necessary

fee simple: a synonym for ownership

finder: a person who locates a buyer or a seller in order to complete a transaction which would probably not take place through ordinary efforts

finder's fee: the amount paid to a finder

firm: strictly speaking, a partnership; however, the term is often applied to corporations as well

first mortgage: a mortgage having priority over all other mortgages on a property. If there is insufficient value in a property to pay off all mortgages, the first mortgage gets paid first, the second mortgage next and so on

fiscal period: the period for which financial statements are prepared, usually the fiscal year

fiscal year: a period of approximately one year for which financial statements are prepared on a regular basis. A fiscal year usually consists of twelve consecutive months but sometimes covers fifty-two or fifty-three consecutive weeks

fixed asset: a tangible long-term asset, such as land, buildings or equipment, held for use rather than for sale

fixed capital: the investment in capital assets

fixed cost: an indirect expense, such as rent, that remains relatively unchanged in total regardless of the volume of production or activity

fixed price contract: a contract under which the contractor receives a fixed amount regardless of his costs of completion

fixture: a fixed asset attached to or forming a normal part of a building

flash report: a preliminary report of estimated earnings issued to top management as soon as possible after the close of an accounting period

float: 1. that portion of a deposit, bank account balance, or of the total deposits of a bank represented by uncollected funds; for example, checks deposited which have not yet been converted to cash by presentation to the bank on which they are drawn 2. the portion of a new issue of securities not yet purchased by the public

floating asset: a current asset

floating charge: debt security in the form of a general claim on the assets of a corporation without attachment to specific assets

floating debt: current liabilities

floating exchange rate: a technique which allows exchange rates in a particular country to float freely allowing that country's currency to find its own level in a free market

floating rate: a variable interest rate

floor: in stock market language, the trading area of an exchange

floor trader: an employee of a member firm of an exchange who trades on the floor of the exchange on behalf of his firm's clients

flotsam: goods from or parts of a shipwrecked vessel which are found floating on the surface of the sea

flow chart: a graphic presentation of the movement in an operational sequence

folio: a page number

foolscap: originally, a piece of paper measuring seventeen inches by thirteen and a half inches. The term is now applied to any sheet of blank paper

force majeure: irresistible force

force sale: an involuntary sale, usually resulting in a price being obtained which is less than fair market value

forecast: a budget

foreclosure: the seizing of property under a mortgage or lien

foreign exchange: a transaction involving the exchange of currency of one country for currency of another

franchise: a privilege under a contract, usually exclusive, permitting the sale of a product, use of a trade name, or provision of a particular service within a specified territory

fraud: a deliberate act of deception or manipulation with the intention of cheating another person or organization

free and clear: in real estate language, property against which there are no encumbrances

free trade: trade between nations with no customs duties or other restrictions imposed

frontage: the linear measurement along the front of a parcel of land such as that fronting on a major road, street, or waterway

front-end loading: the practice of taking from the first instalment payments in respect to the purchase of investments or insurance the amounts required to cover administrative and selling costs, interest, risk and other factors, so that upon early redemption or cancellation the purchaser or investor would receive back little or none of his original cost

functus officio: having discharged one's office or duty

fund: 1. assets set aside for a specific purpose 2. a self-balancing accounting entity

funded debt: long-term debt for which a schedule of repayments has been established

futures: contracts to purchase or sell commodities for future delivery. Such contracts are normally traded on an organized exchange

g

GAAP: abbreviation for generally accepted accounting principles

GAAS: abbreviation for generally accepted auditing standards

GATT: abbreviation for General Agreements on Tariffs and Trade

GNP: abbreviation for gross national product

gain: a monetary profit

garnishee: a person against whom a garnishment is issued

garnishment: a legal proceeding under which a person's salary or other payment due them is taken for payment of a debt by the debtor. A judgment is usually necessary before garnishment is granted

general insurance: insurance other than life insurance

general journal: a book of original entry in which transactions are entered for which specialized journals do not exist

general ledger: a ledger comprising all asset, liability, proprietorship, revenue and expense accounts

generally accepted accounting principles: those accounting principles which have been given formal recognition or authoritative support in a particular jurisdiction

generally accepted auditing standards: those auditing standards which have been given formal recognition or authoritative support in a particular jurisdiction

general price-level accounting: a method of accounting under which assets, liabilities, revenues and expenses are stated in terms of the purchasing power of money at the date of the current financial statements

general strike: a strike by the majority of workers in all the vital industries of a particular locality or region

gilt-edged securities: a synonym for blue chip securities

going concern: a business which is operating and expects to continue operating

going concern concept: the concept that a particular business will continue in operation indefinitely

going concern value: the value of an asset or a business on the assumption of continued use, in contrast to market or liquidation value

gold standard: a monetary standard under which the basic unit of currency of a country is based on a fixed quantity of gold and where such currency is convertible at home or abroad into a fixed amount of gold per unit of currency

goodwill: an intangible asset representing the excess of the total value of the business over the sum of its net identifiable assets

green paper: a publication of a government containing a proposal to which the government has not yet committed itself but on which it would like public comment

Gresham's Law: bad money drives out good

grievance: a complaint against an employer by one or more employees alleging a breach of a collective agreement

gross national product: the market value of the output of goods and services produced by a nation's economy

gross profit: the excess of net sales over the cost of goods sold

ground lease: a lease of vacant land or a lease of land exclusive of any buildings on it

ground rent: rent paid under a ground lease

group insurance: insurance policies taken out on the lives of a particular group, such as the employees of a corporation

growth stock: shares of a corporation which have excellent prospects for future increase in value

guarantee: a contract to discharge the liability or obligation of another person if the latter fails to do so. Sometimes incorrectly used as a synonym for warranty

guaranteed investment certificate: a debt security issued by trust companies, usually in denominations of $5,000 with maturity terms of thirty days to a year or $500 with maturity terms of one to five years

guarantor: a person who provides a guarantee

h

hard copy: printed reports, listings, documents, summaries, etc.

hardware: in computer language, the mechanical, magnetic, electrical and electronic devices, components and equipment of a computer system

head tax: a synonym for poll tax

heavy market: in stock market language, the condition which exists when a large number of selling orders are on the market apparently without sufficient buying orders to balance them off

hedge: to buy or sell futures for the specific purpose of restricting the risk involved in price fluctuations

hidden agenda: matters that are important to an individual attending a meeting but which he cannot raise because the matters are not on the agenda or because they are personal matters relating to the meeting; for example, personal dislike of another attendee at the meeting

hidden tax: a tax which is included in the price of the product and not stated separately

highest and best use: the use of property which will bring the greatest economic return

hire-purchase agreement: a lease containing a purchase option

historical cost: figures based on actual cost

holdback: a portion of a payment called for under a contract which is not payable until certain conditions have been fulfilled

holding company: a corporation whose primary purpose is owning shares of one or more other corporations

holding period: the period during which an asset is owned

holograph: written entirely in one's own handwriting

housing starts: the number of new housing units in residential buildings on which construction has begun

hyperinflation: extreme inflation

hypothecate: to pledge as security

i

ibid.: in the same place

idem: the same

idle capacity: normal capacity which is not being used

imprest fund: a cash fund kept under an imprest system

imprest system: a system for handling disbursements under which a specified amount of cash is entrusted to an individual. The fund is reimbursed periodically for the exact amount of disbursements made from it on the basis of vouchers being presented covering the disbursements. At any particular time, the cash on hand plus the vouchers not reimbursed should equal the amount of the fund

imputed income: income which is not in the form of money, such as free board or lodging, or food produced and consumed by a farmer

imputed interest: interest that is considered to be a cost even though no actual cash outlay is made

income bond: a bond on which the payment of interest is contingent upon earnings

income debenture: a synonym for income bond

incorporation: the legal process of bringing a corporation into existence

in curia: in court

index: a number which measures change in a factor, such as cost of living, from one specific time to another specific time

indenture: a document, deed or contract setting out particular agreements between parties

indicia: indications or signs

indirect cost: an expense that cannot reasonably be identified with a specific operation or cost center

indirect labor: the cost of labor which does not directly affect the composition of a finished product in a manufacturing process

indirect material: the cost of material necessary to the production of a product for sale but not forming an actual part of the final product

indirect overhead: overhead costs which are not traceable to a specific part of a manufacturing operation

indirect tax: a tax that can be shifted from the original payor to the ultimate consumer of the thing taxed; for example, import duties, excise taxes and sales taxes are usually considered to be indirect taxes

in esse: actually existing

in extenso: at full length

inflation: a persistent rise in the economy's general level of prices

infra: below

injunction: a court order to do or not to do a particular thing

in loco parentis: in the place of a parent

in pari materia: in an analogous case or position

in personam: a proceeding against a specific person

in posse: potentially

in potentia: potentially

input: information introduced into a data processing system

in re: in the matter of

in rem: a proceeding

insider: a director or senior officer of a corporation, or anyone who may be presumed to have access to inside information concerning the corporation. Anyone owning more than ten percent of the voting shares of a corporation would likely be deemed an insider in most jurisdictions

insider report: a report of all transactions in the shares of a corporation by those considered to be insiders. This report is required to be submitted on a timely basis to the securities commission within whose jurisdiction the corporation falls

insider trading: transactions in shares of a corporation by insiders

in situ: in position

insolvency: the inability of a person or organization to pay its debts as they become due

instalment sale: a sale in which the price is to be paid by a series of payments over a period of time

in statu quo: in the former position

institutional advertising: advertising intended to promote a favorable opinion of the advertiser rather than any particular product which the advertiser may offer for sale

institutional investor: an institution, such as an insurance company, pension fund or mutual fund, which invests large sums of money in securities

instrument: a written legal document

instrument of incorporation: the legal document by which a corporation is created. Depending on the particular jurisdiction, it could be articles of incorporation, letters patent or a memorandum of association

intangible asset: an asset that lacks physical substance; for example, a copyright, trademark, patent or goodwill

inter alia: among other things

interim audit: the phases of an audit conducted sometime before the end of the accounting period being reviewed

intermediary: a middle man

intermediate goods: goods that enter into the production of other goods

internal audit: an audit of an organization's operations conducted by one or more employees of the organization itself in contrast to an audit conducted by an outside party. It is usually not limited to financial considerations. *See also* **operational audit**

internal auditor: an employee who performs audit functions within an organization

internal control: the plan of organization and the methods adopted by an organization to safeguard its assets and to ensure the accuracy and reliability of accounting data

internal storage: in computer language, storage within the computer system

inter se: between themselves

inter vivos: between living persons

inter-vivos trust: a trust created and coming into existence during the lifetime of the settlor

intestate: without a will

in toto: completely

intra vires: within the power of

inventory: 1. items of tangible property which are held for sale, to be used in the production of goods for sale, or to be consumed in the production of goods or services for sale 2. an itemized list of goods

inventory certificate: a letter of representation obtained by an independent auditor from his client certifying the basis of valuation and the ownership of goods in the inventory

investment club: a group of individuals who pool their funds to invest in securities as a group

investment counselor: one whose profession is giving advice on investments and managing the investments of others for a fee

ipso facto: by that very fact

issue: 1. a matter in dispute 2. the children of a marriage

issued capital: proportion of authorized capital stock for which subscriptions have been received and the stock allotted

jetsam: goods or parts of a ship thrown overboard in order to lighten the vessel

jobber: a wholesaler

job cost system: a method of cost accounting in which costs for distinguishable units are determined by accumulating identifiable costs during the entire production process

joint account: a bank account which may be drawn upon individually by two or more persons

joint and last survivor: provisions in insurance policies and annuities under which the beneficiary accepts a reduced payment for his own and his spouse's lifetime, which upon his death will continue to be paid to his spouse as long as she lives

joint and several: joint and several parties may be sued alone or together as being responsible for the actions of each other

joint tenancy: the state of a land holding in which two or more persons have an undivided interest in the land with equal right to possession and equal title. Upon the death of a joint tenant his rights automatically go to the surviving joint tenant or tenants

joint venture: a business undertaking entered into by two or more parties which is intended to terminate upon the completion of a specific project

journal: a book of original entry

journal entry: an entry in a general journal

journal voucher: a document supporting an entry in a general journal

junior security: a security having a lower priority of claims on assets than another security

key man insurance: life insurance on a key employee, partner or proprietor. The business is the beneficiary under the policy

keypunch: as a noun, the equipment used to record information in cards or tape by punching holes which represent letters, digits and other special characters. As a verb, to operate such a device

kickback: an illegal rebate

kilo: a prefix meaning one thousand

kiting: the act of depositing in one bank account a check drawn on another bank account but recording only the deposit on the day of the transfer. The drawing of the check on the other account is not recorded until a later day with the effect of covering a cash shortage on the day of the actual transfer

LIFO: last in first out

laches: an unreasonable delay by a person in claiming something which is due to him

laissez-faire: the economic theory which states that trade and industry is most profitable when left completely to free enterprise without government intervention or regulation

lead time: the length of time between ordering something and actually receiving it

lease-back: the situation under which the owner of a property sells it to another on condition that the former owner can lease it back for a specified period of time at a specified rent

leasehold improvements: improvements made by a lessee

lease-option agreement: a lease which gives the lessee the option to purchase the subject property at a particular date for a stipulated price

legal tender: money which under the law must be accepted in payment of debts

lessee: one who rents from an owner

lessor: an owner who rents out his property

letter of credit: a letter issued by a bank authorizing the person named therein to draw money up to a specified amount from the bank's branches or correspondents providing the conditions set out in the letter are met

leverage: the condition existing when money is borrowed and reinvested or used to produce a return exceeding the cost of borrowing

liability: something owed

libel: a written derogatory comment

lien: the right to retain possession of another's property until debts owed to the holder of the property are satisfied

life tenant: a person whose interest in property is limited to the duration of his life

limited company: generally speaking, a corporation. The term derives from the fact that the liability of shareholders for debts of the corporation is limited to the amount of capital for which they have subscribed

limited partnership: a partnership consisting of one or more general partners who are financially responsible for losses without limitation and one or more limited partners who contributed a specific amount to the partnership and are liable only up to the amount contributed

line of credit: the stated intention of a lender or supplier to provide credit up to a specified amount

liquid assets: cash and investments which are readily convertible into cash thereby being available for payment of liabilities

liquidation: 1. the conversion of assets into cash 2. the payment of a debt 3. the winding up of a corporation and distribution of its assets to its owners

liquidation value: 1. the amount which an asset might realize upon a forced sale 2. the amount which would be realized upon the winding-up of a business

liquidator: a person appointed to oversee the winding up of the affairs of a corporation or other organization

liquidity: the convertibility of assets into cash

lis pendens: a pending suit

listed securities: securities entitled to trading privileges on a stock exchange

listing: in real estate language, the agreement between the owner of real property and a real estate agent under which the agent agrees to attempt to find a buyer for the property in return for a commission

loading: an amount included in a contracted instalment price to cover administrative and selling costs and interest. It is frequently referred to as finance charges

loan shark: a person who lends money at exorbitant rates of interest

lobby: a person or an organization seeking to influence the proceedings of legislative bodies through personal intervention

lockout: the refusal by an employer to allow employees to work. It usually involves closing the employer's establishments in order to force a settlement in a labor dispute

logo: a distinctive symbol used by an organization to identify itself

long-term asset: long-term investments, fixed assets, and other assets which are not current assets

long-term liability: a liability which in the ordinary course of a business's operation will not be paid within one year

loophole: an ambiguity or omission in a law which allows the intent of the law to be evaded. Sometimes applied to omissions or ambiguities in contracts

loss leader: a product or service which is sold at a loss in order to attract customers who theoretically will then buy other products or services which are profitable

MBO: abbreviation for management by objectives. A management technique designed to achieve overall and individual objectives with all levels of management and staff participating

M.I.M.C.: abbreviation for Member of the Institute of Management Consultants

management consultant: a professional specialist whose business is advising others on management matters

margin: 1. in the brokerage business the term refers to a deposit made with a broker in part payment for securities or commodities to be purchased 2. difference; for example, a margin for profit being the difference between the selling price and all costs in connection with the sale

marginal tax rate: the rate of tax imposed as a percentage of an additional unit of income

margin buying: the purchasing of securities with the aid of credit extended by the purchaser's broker

margin call: the demand made upon a purchaser by his broker for additional sums which may become necessary in order to maintain the required deposit level. *See also* **margin**

marketable security: a security which can be easily sold

marketing boards: government organizations with the power to promote, control and regulate the marketing of natural products; for example, milk or eggs

market value: the prevailing price

maturity: the due date of a security or debt

means test: a method of determining the right of a claimant to a welfare benefit

mediation: in labor language, a synonym for conciliation

mega: a prefix meaning a million

memory: in computer language, a synonym for storage

mens rea: a knowledge of the wrongfulness of an act

merchant bank: a bank whose main business is the lending of money to industry rather than individuals

merger: combination of two or more corporations by the transfer of their assets and liabilities to one of the corporations involved

metes and bounds: the description of land by boundry lines outlining their terminal points and angles

middleman: a person who serves as a link between the producer of goods and the eventual user of the goods

minority interest: common shareholders who neither control a corporation nor form part of a group which controls the corporation

minute book: a book containing the formal minutes of meetings

minutes: a record of the proceedings of a meeting

module: a particular segment of information or a particular piece of equipment

monetary policy: the policy followed by a government for controlling credit and money supply in the economy

money-purchase pension plan: a pension plan under which the benefits are determined by the amount of accumulated contributions allocated to the employee

monopoly: an industry in which there is only one producer and many customers

monopsony: a market in which there are many sellers but only one buyer

moonlighting: when an individual holds more than one job at the same time

moot point: a debatable point

moratorium: a period of suspension of legal rights

mortgage: 1. a legal conveyance of property as security on a loan on condition that the conveyance becomes void when the loan is repaid 2. the instrument by which such a conveyance is made

mortgage bond: a bond which is secured by a mortgage

mortgage broker: a person who, for a fee, brings together borrowers and lenders and handles the necessary documentation

mortgagee: the person who lends money and receives the mortgage

mortgagor: the person who borrows money and gives a mortgage

most-favored-nation clause: a provision in a contract which guarantees one party to the contract treatment no less favorable than that granted by the other party to the contract to other parties under similar contracts

moving average: a statistical term used to indicate an average calculation which is made for a series of figures; for example, if three-month moving average figures are to be calculated on a regular basis the first average would be January, February and March, while the second average calculation would be February, March and April

multi-national: when used in reference to a corporation it normally means one which has investments and business activities in a number of countries

multiple: a synonym for price-earnings ratio

multiple listing: in real estate language, a listing submitted to all members of a real estate association so that each has an opportunity to sell the property; the opposite of an exclusive listing

mutatis mutandis: with the necessary changes

mutual fund: an investment company which sells units or shares to investors. The mutual fund in turn invests in various securities. The concept allows the original investor, by investing in the mutual fund, to diversify his investments or perhaps invest in securities which he could not otherwise afford

national debt: the total amount owed by a federal government

nationalized industry: an industry that has been brought under direct government control and ownership

natural disaster: a synonym for an act of God

naturalization: the granting of citizenship to an alien

negative goodwill: the excess of the book value of a business over the amount paid for it

net assets: the excess of the book value of the assets of an organization over its liabilities

net book value: the portion of the cost of an asset as carried in the records of an organization reflecting the amount which has not yet been written off

net current assets: a synonym for working capital

net lease: a lease under which the tenant agrees to pay, in addition to the rent, expenses such as taxes, insurance, maintenance, etc., of the property leased

net realizable value: selling price less costs of disposal

net worth: a synonym for owners' equity or shareholders' equity

new issue: a stock or bond being sold by a corporation for the first time

nisi: valid unless cause shown for rescinding

nolens volens: whether willing or unwilling

nominal owner: a person who holds title to an asset on behalf of someone else, the latter being the beneficial owner

non-arm's length: a situation in which the parties to a transaction are related or closely connected with each other

non compos mentis: not of sound mind

non-contributory pension plan: a pension plan which is funded completely by employer contributions

non-cumulative stock: a class of preferred stock in which the right to dividends lapses annually; that is, if a dividend is not paid in a particular year it does not get added to the next year's dividend

nondurable goods: goods which generally last for only a short time; for example, food and clothing

non-exclusive listing: in real estate language, a listing under which the real estate agent has an exclusive listing vis-à-vis other real estate agents, but under which the owner may sell the property without using an agent and not be liable to pay a commission to the real estate agent who has the listing

non-profit organization: an organization formed for social, educational, religious or similar purposes and not intended to be operated for profit

non sequitur: illogical inference

no par value stock: shares of capital stock which have no par value

normal capacity: the maximum level of operation under normal circumstances

notary public: a person who is authorized to administer oaths and to attest to the authenticity of signatures

note payable: a liability in the form of a promissory note

note receivable: an asset in the form of a promissory note

nothings: an income tax term which describes expenses which are neither deductible nor depreciable

novation: an agreement to replace an original party to a contract with a new party

nuisance tax: a tax which doesn't produce much revenue but acts as an inconvenience to the taxpayers

numbered account: in banking language, a bank account that is identified by a number only with the name of the account holder being kept secret. Common to Swiss bank accounts

OECD: abbreviation for Organization for Economic Cooperation and Development

OSC: abbreviation for the Ontario Securities Commission

obiter dictum: a judical observation not binding as a precedent

obsolescence: the end of an asset's useful life for reasons other than depreciation or deterioration; for example, a machine becomes obsolete when a new invention renders its use no longer economical

occupational hazard: a risk of injury or sickness that is inherent in certain occupations

odd lot: in stock market language, less than the usual unit of trading; usually fewer than 100 shares of a particular security

officer: a person in a corporation on whom executive authority has been conferred

off-line: in computer language, not under the control of the main computer

off-the-board: a synonym for over-the-counter

oligopoly: a market dominated by a small number of sellers; for example, the automobile manufacturing industry

oligopsony: a market dominated by a small number of buyers

ombudsman: an official whose duty it is to investigate complaints made to him by members of the public against the government

one-write system: a system of bookkeeping in which all records are produced during one operation by the use of reproductive paper and special equipment which properly aligns the documents being processed

on-line: operating directly under control of the main computer

op. cit.: in the work or works cited

open account: a credit term indicating an unsecured amount

open-end: the term describing the capital structure of an organization whose shares or units are not transferable but may be redeemed at the sole option of the shareholder or unit holder. The opposite of closed-end

open-end fund: a synonym for a mutual fund

open market: a freely competitive market in which buyers and sellers need not be members of a particular exchange or group and in which there is no particular location for trading

open shop: the situation where some employees in a bargaining unit are members of a union and others are not

operating company: a company which is actively engaged in the operation of a business in contrast to a holding company which simply invests in other companies

operating cycle: the time period between the acquisition of raw materials or merchandise and the receipt of cash from their sale

operational audit: an examination of an organization's operating structure, policies, and systems and procedures with a view to assessing their effectiveness and efficiency

opportunity cost: the value of benefits given up by virtue of selecting a particular course of action

ordinary creditor: an unsecured creditor

ordinary stock: a synonym for common stock

organization expense: the cost of forming or incorporating an organization

Organization for Economic Cooperation and Development: an international, intergovernmental organization designed to contribute to sound economic expansion and development. Its members are: Austria, Belgium, Canada, Denmark, France, the Federal Republic of Germany, Greece, Iceland, Ireland, Italy, Luxembourg, the Netherlands, Norway, Portugal, Spain, Sweden, Switzerland, Turkey, the United Kingdom and the United States

out-of-pocket cost: an expense incurred on behalf of another for which reimbursement will be sought

output: 1. information produced by a data processing system 2. the quantity of goods or services produced

outstanding: unpaid, uncleared, unredeemed or unfilled depending upon the noun with which the term is used

overdraft: the situation existing when withdrawals exceed deposits

overhead: expenses incurred to operate a business but which cannot conveniently be attributed to individual units of production or service

over-the-counter: transactions in securities or commodities which are not listed on a stock or commodity exchange

over-the-counter sale: the sale of an unlisted security

owners' equity: a synonym for net assets or shareholders' equity

paid-in surplus: a synonym for contributed surplus

paid-up capital: issued capital which has been paid for

paper profit: an unrealized profit

parameter: a definable characteristic

parent company: a corporation which controls one or more other corporations through ownership of a majority of the voting shares

pari passu: equally

Parkinson's Law: the theory that work expands to fill the time available

parol: not written

participating stock: a class of preferred stock which will carry a dividend not less than that paid on the common stock; sometimes participating stock will also share in the residual distribution on liquidation of a corporation

partnership: two or more persons engaged in a business with a view to making a profit

par value: the face value of a security

passim: in various places

past service pension cost: the pension cost relating to an employee's employment before a pension plan is put into effect

past service pension liability: the present value of the cost of unpaid past service pension benefits

patent: the authority given by a government to a first inventor to enjoy the exclusive benefits from the invention for a particular period, usually seventeen years

patronage dividend: a distribution to customers based on the volume of business done with each customer over a period of time

pawnbroker: a person who is licensed to lend money upon the security of valuable goods left with him until the loan is repaid

payback period: the estimated period of time over which the cash flow from an investment or project will equal its original cost

payment in kind: payment in the form of goods or services rather than money

payola: bribery

peculation: the embezzlement of public funds by a person in whose care they have been entrusted

pegging: the manipulation of the price of something so that it remains stationary or within very narrow ranges

penalty clause: a provision in a contract requiring one party to pay a sum of money to the other if the contract is not kept

penny stocks: low-priced shares, usually speculative, normally applied to stock selling at less than one dollar per share

pension: a benefit paid to a retired employee

pension fund: the cash, investments and other assets set aside for the payment of pensions

pension plan: the arrangement under which pensions are paid

peppercorn rent: a small nominal rent

per annum: yearly

per capita: for each person

percentage-of-completion method: an accounting method under which income is recognized proportionately to the degree of completion of a contract

per curiam: by the court

per diem: daily

performance bond: a bond posted to ensure completion

period costs: costs charged off as expenses in the period in which they are incurred rather than included in inventory

per se: by itself

per stirpes: by the number of families

petty cash: a cash fund kept on hand as a convenience in making small payments

phantom stock plan: a bonus arrangement under which an employee is paid an amount determined by the rise in value of the employer's stock over a specified period of time even though the employee does not actually acquire any shares of the stock

planned obsolescence: periodic changes in the design of products so that consumers are induced to buy new ones before the old ones have worn out. The most common example is the automobile industry

plenary session: a session of a conference which all delegates attend

poll tax: a tax applied equally to every individual required to pay it regardless of personal income or assets

portfolio investments: long-term investments in corporations which are not subsidiaries

possession: the condition of being in physical control of property whether or not the property is owned by the person having the control. Possession can be lawful or unlawful

post: to transfer an amount from a book of original entry to a ledger or from a source document to a book of original entry

postdate: a document or check that is dated some time in the future

pound sterling: the term used to distinguish the British pound from the pounds of other countries

power of attorney: an authorization in writing given by one person to another enabling the latter to act on behalf of the former in respect to specific matters or in general

preferred creditor: a person who, by law, is entitled to full satisfaction of his claim against the estate of a bankrupt before other unsecured creditors receive anything

preferred stock: a class of capital stock with special rights or restrictions. The preference usually refers to the distribution of dividends at a fixed annual rate. Sometimes the preference refers to a priority for a return of capital upon liquidation of the corporation. The restrictions usually apply to voting rights: usually preferred stock only carries votes when dividends are in arrears

premium: the amount by which the selling price of a security exceeds its par value

present value: the discounted value, assuming a given rate of interest over a given period of time

press kit: prepared information given to journalists at a press conference

price-earnings ratio: the market price of a share of common stock of a corporation divided by the annual earnings per share for the preceeding period

price war: a systematic reduction in the price of a commodity or service by two or more competing firms

prima facie: on first sight

primary distribution: the original sale of any issue of a corporation's securities

prime costing: a method of cost accounting in which both fixed and variable overhead expenses are regarded as period costs and excluded from inventory valuation

prime rate: the interest rate charged by banks to its preferential borrowers. The lowest rate of interest available to borrowers

principal: 1. a person who employs another person (called the agent) to act on his behalf with third persons 2. a sum on which interest is earned or paid

printout: the output of a computer, usually produced on continuously moving paper

private company: generally speaking, a corporation whose shares are not listed or traded on a recognized stock exchange or otherwise available to the public

private ledger: an accounting ledger in which selected confidential accounts are kept

private sector: the sector of an economy that consists of individuals, corporations, firms and other institutions that are not under government control

probate: to prove a will in court

process cost system: a method of cost accounting in which costs for nondistinguishable units of production are determined by accumulating the costs of the total production process over a period of time and dividing the result by the number of units produced

profit center: a unit of a business that is accountable for specific revenues and expenses

profiteer: a person who takes advantage of a shortage of goods

profit-sharing plan: a plan under which an employer makes bonuses available to employees, either currently or on a deferred basis, based on the profit of the business

profit taking: the process of converting paper profits into cash by selling the securities

pro forma: for illustrative purposes

program: a detailed sequence of instructions a computer performs in order to solve a problem

progressive tax: a tax in which the average amount payable increases with the size of the tax base

proletariat: the working class

proposal: a suggestion for an extension of time or a reduction in the amount of debt put forward to creditors by a debtor

proprio motu: of one's own accord

pro rata: proportionally

prospectus: a complex document issued by a corporation or promoter in connection with the offering of securities or other investment opportunities containing specific information about the offeror's business, the type of investment, financial data and other pertinent facts in conformity with security regulations

pro tanto: to that extent

pro tem: temporarily

protocol: a formal code of etiquette

proviso: a condition

proxy: 1. a person with authority in writing to vote in the place of another 2. the instrument of proxy itself

proxy battle: a contest between two or more factions in a corporation in which each faction seeks to gain control of enough proxies to enable it to elect its candidates to the board of directors or win a decision in a vote

public company: a corporation whose shares are available to the public

public sector: the sector of an economy consisting of all government-owned institutions

purchase order: a form used to order goods or services

put: a transferable option to sell a given number of shares of a particular stock at a stated price during a particular period of time

pyramid selling: a method of selling under which a central organization recruits a small number of regional organizers who in turn recruit a number of subdistributors who in turn recruit salesmen who, at the bottom of the pyramid, normally end up selling the goods door-to-door

q

qua: in the capacity of

qualifying share: a share of a corporation held by an individual in order to qualify as a director

quantum meruit: as much as he has earned

quick ratio: the ratio of the total cash, accounts receivable, and marketable securities to current liabilities

quid pro quo: something given for something else

quiet enjoyment: uninterrupted use and possession

quitclaim: a release

quoad: as regards; as far as

quorum: the number of persons who must legally be present at a meeting in order to effectively transact business

r

R & D: abbreviation for research and development

R.I.A.: abbreviation for Registered Industrial Accountant

r.o.i.: return on investment; in other words, the annual profit resulting from an investment, usually expressed as a percentage of the investment

rally: in stock market language, a brisk rise in prices following a decline in the general price level of the market as a whole or in an individual stock

random access: in computer language, the ability to extract information without the necessity of searching through the stored information to obtain the data

random sample: a sample in which all the elements have been drawn according to the laws of chance

rate card: standard charges for advertising

ratio decidendi: the reasons for a judicial decision

raw land: land which has not been subdivided into lots, does not have water, sewers, streets, utilities or other improvements

raw material: material acquired for the purpose of being changed in form or consumed in a manufacturing process

re: in the matter of

real estate: immovable property such as land and buildings

real estate investment trust: an investment company that specializes in the real estate field, investing either in mortgages or in real property or a combination of both

realtor: a real estate agent who is a member of a real estate board

rebate: the return of part of a payment for goods or services in contrast to a discount which is deducted in advance

receiver: a person appointed by a court or a creditor to take charge of property pending the final decision of the matter either in the courts or by payment in full of the debt owed to the creditor

receivership: the legal status of a debtor for whom a person has been appointed by the court (or sometimes appointed by a creditor) to take charge of the debtor's relevant affairs pending payment of the debt or other disposition of the matter by the courts

recession: a decline in overall business activity

reciprocity: a form of tariff agreement under which nations agree to extend to each other any reduction in import tariffs made by one of them

record date: the date on which a person must be registered on the books of a corporation as a shareholder in order to receive a dividend declared or to vote on the company's affairs

recovery: an increase in business activity after a recession

redeemable stock: a class of capital stock which can be redeemed at the option of the corporation

red-herring prospectus: a preliminary prospectus

redistribution of income: a government policy under which large incomes are reduced through progressive taxation of income and wealth

Regina: reigning queen

registrar: the person responsible for the maintenance of a corporation's shareholders' and bondholders' records

regressive tax: a tax whose average rate declines as the tax base increases

reinsurance: a contract between insurers whereby one assumes some of the risk (sometimes all) on an insurance contract issued by the other

REIT: abbreviation for real estate investment trust

remainderman: the person entitled to the remainder after a life interest has been extinquished

repatriation: the transfer of capital from foreign countries back to one's home country

replevin: a legal action to recover goods wrongfully taken in situations where damages are not satisfactory

repudiation: the refusal to fulfill a contract or pay a debt

rescind: to void or cancel a contract or a term thereof as if the object of the rescission had never existed

reserve: an amount appropriated for accounting purposes from retained earnings or other surplus, at the discretion of management or pursuant to the requirements of law or an agreement, for a specific or general purpose. The existence of a reserve indicates that an unidentified portion of the organization's assets is being held for general or specific purposes

reserve bid: in an auction, a price below which the auctioneer is not permitted to sell an item

residue: in the language of wills, the property of a deceased after all expenses of administration and all specific bequests have been paid

res inter alios acta: a transaction between other parties

res ipsa loquitur: the thing speaks for itself

res judicata: a case already settled

res nova: a matter not yet decided

restitutio in integrum: restoration to the original position

retained earnings: the accumulated balance of profits less losses of a corporation as adjusted for dividends and other appropriate charges or credits

reverse takeover: a term usually applied to a situation where ownership of a larger company is acquired by a smaller company. It usually requires an extensive reorganization of the acquiring company's capitalization

revolving credit: an arrangement which permits a purchaser to charge purchases against an account every month provided the balance does not exceed a predetermined credit limit. Monthly payments must be made on the account

Rex: reigning king

rider: something added to a contract

right: *See* **rights issue**

right-of-way: the right of one person to pass over another's land

rights issue: the issue by a corporation to its existing shareholders of the right to purchase new shares in the same proportion as that in which the shareholders already own existing shares. A shareholder who does not wish to accept the shares may sell some or all of his rights to another person

rolling stock: a term applied to railroad engines and cars

royalty: a payment made for the right to use another person's property for purposes of gain

run on a bank: a mass withdrawal of deposits from a bank by depositers who no longer have confidence that the bank has sufficient funds to pay off all depositers

S

SEC: abbreviation for the Securities and Exchange Commission in the United States

S.M.A.: abbreviation for Society of Management Accountants

sale and leaseback: the sale of an asset with the vendor immediately renting the asset from the purchaser for long-term use

sales journal: a book of original entry in which sales are recorded

salvage value: scrap value

savings certificate: a debt security issued by banks in denominations of ten dollars to one hundred dollars with a maturity term of up to six years. It is normally issued at a discount

scab: a strikebreaker

scrip: a certificate which is exchangeable for stock or cash before a specified date and after which it may well have no value

seal: a physical impression made on a document to attest to a signature or to add to its formality

seasonally adjusted: an annual rate for which data have been adjusted for seasonal variation and then expressed as if the same level of performance as that for the reported period will continue for the entire year

seat: membership in a stock exchange

secondary distribution: the re-distribution to the public of a significant number of shares of the corporation which had previously been distributed to the public

secret reserves: the accounting term applied to reserves kept by a company but not disclosed in its financial statements. This condition is achieved by wrongfully valuing assets or liabilities; for example, over-depreciating assets

sector: a division of an economy which has characteristics allowing it to be studied in isolation from the rest of the economy

secured creditor: a person whose claim against a debtor is supported by assets which have been pledged to the creditor by the debtor or upon which the creditor has a lien

security: 1. a share certificate, bond, debenture or other document evidencing debt or ownership 2. property pledged to secure performance of a contract or payment of a debt

self-insurance: the assumption by the insured of a risk which might otherwise have been covered by insurance; for example, only covering seventy-five percent of a possible loss with insurance on the basis that it would be cheaper to absorb the remaining twenty-five percent loss than pay the premiums required for full coverage

sellers' market: when demand exceeds supply

senior debt: debt that has a higher priority of claims than other debts

senior security: a security that has a higher priority of claims than other securities

serial bond: an issue of bonds redeemable in periodical installments

settlement date: 1. the date on which stock exchange transactions are due for delivery and payment 2. any date on which payment for goods or services is made

settlor: one who creates a trust

severance pay: a payment made to an employee whose employment is prematurely terminated through no fault of his own

shared time: in computer language, the condition under which more than one customer shares access to a computer system

shareholder: the legal owner of shares of a corporation

shareholder of record: a shareholder in whose name shares are registered in the share register of a corporation

shareholders' deficiency: the excess of liabilities over assets of a corporation; the opposite of shareholders' equity

shareholders' equity: the excess of assets over liabilities of a corporation

shop steward: the key individual in the handling of day-to-day grievances in a union

short sale: the sale of a security or commodity not owned by the seller at the time of the sale in the hope that the security or commodity can be purchased at a lower price before the settlement date

sic: it was stated thusly

sight draft: a bill of exchange payable three days after presentation

signing officer: an officer of an organization authorized to sign documents on behalf of the organization

silent partner: a partner who provides money to a partnership but takes no active part in its management or operation

sine die: without a day being named

sine qua non: indispensable condition or qualification

sinking fund: a pool of cash and investments earmarked to provide resources for the redemption of debt or capital stock

sinking fund reserve: the portion of retained earnings appropriated for the purposes of establishing a sinking fund

situs: location

slander: defamation through words; often restricted to written words

slump: in stock market language, a sudden drop in prices or a lessening of business activity

social accounting: the identification, classification, measurement and reporting of the social costs and benefits of human activity in and of an organization

sole proprietorship: an unincorporated business owned by one person

solvency: the ability to pay debts as they become due

solvent: financially able to pay one's current debts

source document: an original record of a transaction

specific performance: a legal action to compel performance under a contract when damages for breach of contract would be unsatisfactory

speculator: an investor who deals in risk and uncertainty

spouse: one's wife or husband

spread: 1. the excess of the selling price over direct costs; the gross profit percentage 2. the range between the bid and ask prices of a stock or commodity

stale-dated check: a check which has not been presented to the bank for payment within a reasonable time, generally six months

standard costing: a method of cost accounting in which costs of production are recorded on the basis of predetermined standards with a view to achieving cost control through analysis of variances between actual and standard conditions

standing loan: a loan requiring payments of interest only, the principal being paid in full upon maturity

stare decisis: to abide by authorities or cases already decided

status quo: the existing state of things at a given time

statutory audit: an audit carried out to comply with the provisions of a statute

stipend: a synonym for salary

stock dividend: a dividend paid by the issue of additional shares of capital stock

stockholder: a synonym for shareholder

stock option: the right to purchase shares of a corporation's capital stock under fixed conditions concerning number of shares, price and time. Such rights are usually given to officers and employees of the corporation

stock split: the division of the outstanding shares of a corporation into a larger number of shares without a change in value of the total shares outstanding; for example, one $500 share might be replaced by fifty shares each worth $10

stop-loss order: an order for the purchase and sale of securities or commodities designed to take affect as soon as the market price of the security or commodity reaches a specified amount

stop payment: instructions given to a bank by the drawer of a check not to honor it

straddle: the purchase of both a put and a call for a single security at the same market price

straight-line method: a method of depreciation calculation in which the periodic charge is computed by dividing the depreciation base by the estimated number of periods of useful life; for example, for an asset having an estimated life of five years, one-fifth would be written off each year

strap: in stock market language, a combination of one put and two calls

street certificate: a stock certificate registered in the name of an investment dealer rather than in the name of the individual owner. This procedure makes it easier to negotiate sales of the particular shares. *See also* **bearer security**

street form: *See* **street certificate**

strikebreaker: a person who replaces workers who are on strike

strip: in stock market language, a combination of one call and two puts

sub judice: under consideration

sublease: an agreement under which a tenant transfers all or part of his rights under a lease to another person

sub modo: under condition or restriction

sub nom: under the name of

subordinate debt: debt that has a lower priority of claims than other debts

subpoena: the legal process under which the appearance of a person or documents in court is required

subrogation: the substitution of one person for another

subsidiary company: a corporation in which another corporation owns a majority of the voting shares

subsidiary ledger: a ledger in which individual accounts of the same type are kept with the aggregate of the accounts being maintained in the control account in the general ledger

subsidy: a payment made by a government to prevent an increase in the price of a product

sui generis: of its own peculiar kind

sui juris: of his own right; such as being of full age and capacity

sum-of-the-years'-digits method: a method of calculating depreciation in which the depreciation base is allocated to individual years on a reducing basis by multiplying the base by a fraction in which the numerator is the number of years plus one of the estimated life remaining and the denominator is the sum of the series of numbers representing the years in the total estimated life; for example, for an asset having an estimated life of five years the denominator is 15 (being $1+2+3+4+5$) and the numerator for the first year would be 5, for the second year 4, and so on

supra: above

surcharge: a charge imposed on top of an existing charge

surety: a person who agrees to satisfy the obligation of another

surplus: the excess of assets over the aggregate of liabilities and capital of a corporation

surrogate: a substitute

surtax: a tax added on an item which is already taxed; usually a percentage of the existing tax

suspense account: an account to which an entry is posted until its ultimate disposition is decided upon

swings: in stock market language, up and down price movements

synergy: the condition under which combined activity is more effective than the total of the independent activities

t

take out loan: the long-term financing of a real estate project after completion of construction

takeover bid: a bid to purchase shares of a corporation with a view to gaining control of the corporation

task force: a small group organized to attain a specific objective

tax avoidance: the minimizing of one's liability for tax by legal means

tax base: the measure upon which the amount of a tax liability is determined

tax burden: the amount of tax actually paid by a taxpayer

tax evasion: the minimizing of one's liability for tax by illegal means

tax haven: a political jurisdiction which levies little or no income or death taxes

tax roll: a list published by a political subdivision containing the descriptions of all land in the subdivision, the names of the owners, the assessed value of the properties and the amount of taxes thereon

tax sale: a public sale of property at auction by a governmental authority after a period of nonpayment of tax

tax shelter: a situation in which deductions for tax purposes are created without a corresponding decrease in cash flow

technical rally: a rally on a stock exchange brought about by an excess of buyers over sellers

tenants in common: two or more persons holding real property each with an undivided interest which may be transferred by alienation or devised by will but for which there are no rights of survivorship. Contrast with joint tenants

term deposit receipt: a debt security issued by a bank, normally in denominations of $5,000, with maturity terms from thirty days to one year

term insurance: an insurance policy for a limited period of time under which the insured must die before the insurer pays any benefits. If the insured outlives the term he receives nothing

term loan: a loan for a stated period of time

testament: a will

testamentary trust: a trust created upon the death of a person through his will

testator: a person who has made a will

thin capitalization: the state of having a high debt to equity ratio

thin market: a market in which there are very few buyers or sellers or both

third party: a person who is not directly involved in a matter

tight money: money that can be borrowed only at very high interest rates

time deposit: a deposit in a financial institution for a specific minimum period of time

time is of the essence: a clause included in contracts to bind one party to performance at or by a specified time in order to bind the other party to its performance

tip: in stock market language, supposedly inside information

title: the evidence that one has a right of possession to real property

title insurance: a bond of indemnity guaranteeing that a recorded instrument, such as a deed, is genuine

title search: a review of all the recorded documents affecting a particular piece of real estate to determine the present condition of title

top hat pension: a pension plan whose membership is restricted to senior executives or owners of a corporation

tort: a civil wrong committed against a person independent of any contractual agreement or criminal action

tract: a parcel of land

trade discount: a deduction from the list price of goods given to particular types of purchasers

trademark: a mark, usually registered, used to show that a particular article is manufactured by a certain firm or organization

transfer agent: the agent of a corporation responsible for the issue, recording, and cancellation of its share certificates and bonds

transfer payment: a payment made by a government which is not in exchange for goods or services, such as old age pensions, family allowances, unemployment insurance, etc.

transfer tax: a tax levied on a transfer of securities or land; usually expressed as a percentage of the transfer price

treasury shares: authorized but unissued shares

trespass: the wrongful entry of one person onto another's property

trial balance: a list of all account balances in a ledger prepared to determine whether the ledger is in balance

trustee: a person who holds title to property for the benefit of another

trustee in bankruptcy: a person appointed by a court to administer the estate of a bankrupt and ultimately distribute the available assets to creditors

turn key: in real estate language, the condition under which property is ready for occupation by literally "turning the key" in the door. In other words, everything is provided except furniture

tycoon: a person who has accumulated great wealth in industry or commerce

ultra vires: beyond the power; in excess of the authority conferred by law

underdeveloped nation: a country in which the per capita income is relatively low in comparison to that of industrial nations

underwriter: a company who accepts an insurance risk

undivided interest: an interest by two or more people in the same property without identification of the parts of the property which belong to the respective parties

unfunded pension plan: a pension plan under which no pension fund has been set up

unimproved land: in real estate language, usually used to indicate land without buildings, although sometimes it is used as a synonym for raw land

union shop: where employees in a bargaining unit must become and remain members of the union. New employees must join the union after a certain number of days

unit benefit pension plan: a synonym for benefit-based pension plan

upset price: the lowest price at which a seller is willing to sell

usufruct: the right to use another person's property without the right to diminish it or damage it

usury: interest charged at a rate higher than that which is permitted by law

uttering: using a forged document with the knowledge that it is forged

v.a.t.: abbreviation for value added tax

valuable consideration: a legal term meaning any consideration sufficient to support a contract. The consideration given does not have to be of equal value to the consideration received under the contract, nor does the term mean great value, but rather merely having value

value added tax: a tax levied at each stage in the production and distribution chain of a product based on the value that is added to the product as it passes through that stage

variable interest rate: an interest rate which moves up and down as the prevailing prime rate of interest fluctuates

venue: the geographical legal jurisdiction in which an action or prosecution is brought for trial. The venue may be changed in criminal cases where local prejudice seems unavoidable

vest: to obtain absolute ownership

vide: see; used to direct a reader to another item

void: having no force or effect

voidable: capable of being either confirmed or being void

volume discount: a reduction in the selling price of goods or services in consideration of large purchases over a particular period of time

voluntary arbitration: arbitration agreed to by the parties to a dispute without statutory compulsion

voting trust: an agreement among shareholders of a corporation whereby their votes are to be cast by a trustee in the interests of the entire group

warrant: a certificate giving the holder the right to purchase securities at a specific price within a specific period of time

warranty: essentially a guarantee that a thing which is sold will be suitable for the purpose for which the purchaser intends to use it

wash sale: a sale which is immediately counterbalanced by a purchase with the result that the sale was a fiction

wasting assets: natural resources which are subject to depeletion, such as timber or mineral deposits

watered stock: shares which a corporation issues without receiving full payment for them. Illegal in most jurisdictions

wear and tear: the loss in value of a property caused by its normal and reasonable use

welfare state: a democratic state with comprehensive social services

white-collar workers: the term applied to office and professional personnel in contrast to production and maintenance workers

white paper: a government publication containing a statement of policy which it expects to enact into law

window dressing: lawful manipulation designed to show something in its most favorable light

withholding tax: a tax deducted at source

without prejudice: effective only when used by legal counsel, it is a term to describe a statement given on the understanding that it cannot be construed as an admission of liability nor can it be admitted in evidence. Such statements are made in attempts to settle disputes out of court

without recourse: a phrase indicating that the holder of a document has no recourse to the person from whom he obtained it

working capital: the excess of current assets over current liabilities

working capital ratio: a synonym for current ratio

work-in-progress: partly finished goods or contracts which are in the process of manufacture or completion at the end of an accounting period or at any particular time

wrap-around mortgage: a second mortgage with a face value equal to the amount it covers and the balance due under the first mortgage. The second mortgagee collects payments based on the face value of the wrap-around mortgage and then pays off the first mortgagee

year-end audit: the phases of an audit conducted at and after the end of the accounting period being reviewed

yellow dog contract: an employment arrangement under which an employee promises that he will not join a union

yield: a synonym for effective rate

Z

zero-base budgeting: a system of budgeting under which all expenditures are reevaluated every time a new budget is prepared. No program is automatically carried forward

zip code: the U.S. postal code

zoning: in real estate language, the division of a political subdivision by legislative regulation into various zones with specifications as to the uses to which real property in the particular zones may be put